D1150276

Talking about Jesus without Sounding Religious

Rebecca Manley Pippert

InterVarsity Press
Downers Grove, Illinois
Leicester, England

InterVarsity Press
P.O. Box 1400, Downers Grove, IL 60515-1426
World Wide Web: www.ivpress.com
E-mail: mail@ivpress.com

Inter-Varsity Press, England
38 De Montfort Street, Leicester LE1 7GP, England
World Wide Web: www.ivpbooks.com
E-mail: ivp@uccf.org.uk

InterVarsity Press® is the book-publishing division of InterVarsity Christian Fellowship/USA®, a student movement active on campus at hundreds of universities, colleges and schools of nursing in the United States of America, and a member movement of the International Fellowship of Evangelical Students. For information about local and regional activities, write Public Relations Dept., InterVarsity Christian Fellowship/USA, 6400 Schroeder Rd., P.O. Box 7895, Madison, WI 53707-7895, or visit the IVCF website at <www.ivcf.org>.

Inter-Varsity Press, England, is the book-publishing division of the Universities and Colleges Christian Fellowship (formerly the Inter-Varsity Fellowship), a student movement linking Christian Unions in universities and colleges throughout the United Kingdom and the Republic of Ireland, and a member movement of the International Fellowship of Evangelical Students. For information about local and national activities write to UCCF, 38 De Montfort Street, Leicester LE1 7GP.

Portions of this book were originally published as Pizza Parlor Evangelism.

The story on pages 44-46 is adapted from Out of the Saltshaker.

Cover design: Cindy Kiple

Cover and interior image: Steve Cole/Getty Images

U.S. ISBN 0-8308-2123-6

U.K. ISBN 0 85111-788-0

Printed in the United States of America ∞

P	15	14	13	12	11	10	9	8	7	6	5	4	3	2	1
Y	13	12	11	10	09	08	07	06	05	04	03				

To Ruth Siemens,

My mentor, my friend and

a true hero of the faith,

whose life has shaped not only mine

but countless others around the world.

I dedicate this series to you—

with gratitude beyond expression.

It was a beautiful spring day in Chicago. The windows of my car were down, and my senses were delighting in the first signs of spring. Just as the light turned green, something suddenly came spiraling into my window and hit me on the cheek. It didn't hurt so much as startle me. I quickly pulled into the gas station to investigate what it was. To my astonishment as I unrolled the paper I discovered it was a gospel tract! Then I remembered having seen a woman in the car next to me whose face bore this strange expression—as if she was anxiously measuring the distance of something.

Is This Evangelism?

The heart of evangelism is sharing the story of Christ, the good news of how God, through Christ, took the sin and shame of the human race so that all who believe might be saved. Acts 4:12 tells us, "There is salvation in no one else, for there is no other name under heaven given among mortals by which we must be saved" (NRSV). This is the most liberating news ever to grace our planet. So why aren't we more eager to share it? Perhaps it is because we have seen poor examples of evangelism—like the one above.

I am sure this woman was a very sincere Christian. I bet she even had daily devotions. However,

I can't ever recall seeing "torpedo evangelism" practiced in the Bible! As I rolled out the tract, I couldn't help but note the paradox. The dilemma I faced in the car was that while the truth expressed in that gospel tract was the most glorious and life-changing news to ever grace our planet, the style of communicating that truth was so abysmal that the message was nearly obliterated.

Some of us may secretly fear that effective evangelism begins with the question "How many people am I supposed to offend this week?" A tension begins to build inside. "Should I be sensitive to people and forget about evangelism, or should I blast them with the gospel and forget about their humanity?" Many Christians choose to be aware of the person but then feel defensive and guilty for not evangelizing. There is something wrong with this concept of evangelism.

Whenever I speak on the topic of evangelism, I always sense that people are breathlessly waiting for the new, argument-proof, jelled approach— the magic formula that works on one and all or your money back. But even if I had such a formula to sell, it still would not work. Our problem in evangelism is not that we do not have enough information; it's that *we do not know how to be ourselves.* We have not grasped that it really is okay for us to be who we are when we are with non-

Christians, even if we do not have all the answers to their questions or if our knowledge of Scripture is limited. We forget that we are called to be witnesses to what we have seen and what we know, not to what we do not know. The key is obedience, not earning an academic degree in theology.

But there is a deeper problem here. Our uneasiness with non-Christians reflects our uneasiness with our own humanity. Because we are not certain about what it means to be human (or spiritual, for that matter), we struggle in relating naturally, humanly, to the world. For example, many of us avoid evangelism for fear that we will offend someone. Yet how often have we told a non-Christian that is why we are hesitating?

I have every right to say, "Look, I'm really excited about sharing with you who God is. But I also know that I hate it when people push 'religion' on me, so if I come on too strong will you tell me?" By saying this, I am communicating that we have a great deal in common: I do not want to dump the gospel, and he or she does not want to be dumped on. So on the basis of this common human bond, I am freed to share my faith.

Self-Discovery

God has given me increasing freedom to talk about him to others. But it has not always been that way.

One day in college I reflected on my evangelistic ministry and realized that, although I had lots of non-Christian friends and some had become Christians through my influence, no one had ever become a Christian in my presence. As I pondered why I still felt uncomfortable about evangelism, I discovered several things about myself.

First, I was so afraid of being identified as a religious weirdo or a Jesus freak that I often remained silent when the topic of God came up. How people saw me mattered more than how God saw me. Ironically, in reality most people respect and respond to a person who has definite ideas and who communicates them clearly rather than someone who seems apologetic and wishy-washy.

Second, although I saw the needs in the lives of my non-Christian friends, I could not imagine that it was Jesus Christ whom they were really searching for. Jesus was for "religious folk," not for my pagan friends. So because I never really expected them to respond to the gospel, they did not.

Third, I feared that Jesus was just *my* way of life. Wasn't it arrogant to suggest that *my* view was the only way? But as I grew to understand the nature of Christianity, I saw that our faith stands on historical fact, not merely subjective experience. Truth—not a feeling in my heart—was the issue. God was not asking me to stand on my own ideas or emotions but on the very person and work of Jesus Christ. If anyone was guilty of being offensive, it was Jesus—not me. It was *his* idea that he was the only way to God, not mine. This realization freed me when I was accused of being narrow. I could answer, "Isn't it amazing that Jesus actually said so many narrow things? Wouldn't it be intriguing to study him to discover why he made such radical claims?"

Next, I was paralyzed by fear that I would offend people and forever ruin their chances of entering the kingdom. So I thought, *I'll just be nice and smile and hope they catch on.* Oddly enough, I have since discovered that offending people is rarely a problem in evangelism. If you are sensitive enough to realize that you might offend someone, then it is usually not your problem.

Also, I could not talk about God in a natural way. I was fine until the topic of "religion" came up. Suddenly I felt as if I needed to sound "spiritual," and instead of listening, I would panic because I could not remember any Scripture verses. My hands would get clammy; my eyes would dart from side to side, hoping no one else was listening; the tone of my voice would change, and I would begin talking "religiously." And then I would wonder why people always looked so uncomfortable when we talked about spiritual things! My problem was that I did not think God could be a natural, integrated part of an ongoing discussion about films, politics or whatever book I was currently reading. I did not have an integrated Christian worldview; God was compartmentalized and separated from "normal" living.

And finally, no one ever became a Christian through me because I never asked them to! Why? Because I was petrified that if I brought someone to the point of becoming a Christian, God would not come through. My fear was that when I would witness to someone, nothing I said would make sense. I would be out there on a limb with no celestial backup. That would put me in an embarrassing situation, so I avoided taking the risk.

Then everything changed. An atheist friend of mine completely amazed me by becoming a Christian. I began to make some startling discoveries when she told me how she had felt before accepting Christ.

"At first I thought, *Fine, let Becky have her religion—that's her thing. I'm not the least bit interested, but if that's what she likes, then it's all right with me.* When you invited me to dinner, you asked if we could thank God for the food. I thought, *Oh, how quaint.* Only you didn't just thank him for the food—you thanked him for *me* and our friendship! It made me feel so good. I never thought you felt our relationship had anything to do with God. But then I thought, *That's ridiculous—thanking someone who doesn't exist for me.*

"Then we went to a film that raised some thoughtful questions, and afterward you said the same central idea of the film was also in a Bible passage you had read and been reflecting on that day. I never dreamed God would have anything remotely in common with modern cinema! Another day you invited me to an objective, no-strings-attached study of the person of Jesus in the Bible. Fine. Only the trouble was—I found I was drawn to this Jesus! He seemed so real and wise as we would read about him each week.

"But you know what affected me most? All my life I used to think, *How arrogant for someone to call himself a Christian, to think he's that good.* But then I got to know you—and Becky, you are far from perfect, yet you call yourself a Christian. So my first shock was to discover you make mistakes like I do. But the biggest shock was that you admitted it, when I couldn't. Suddenly I saw that being a Christian didn't mean never failing, but admitting when you've failed. I wanted to keep Christ in a box and let you be religious during Bible studies. But the more you let me inside your life—and the more I knew the real you, with the problems and joys—the more impossible it became to keep the lid on Christianity. Even your admission of weaknesses drove me to him!"

That confession changed my life. What amazed me was that she had seen me in all kinds of circumstances—she had seen the real me—and it gave the gospel *more* power, not less. I had always thought I should cover up my doubts and problems, because if she really knew me she would not become a Christian. But the more real and transparent I was (even with my weaknesses), the more real Jesus Christ became to her.

Now please get this straight. By saying we must be human with each other, I am not condoning sin. God's call is to moral purity and wholeness. I am not suggesting we share our weaknesses as if being real is a competitive sinning match. Sin is not God's brand of humanity; obedience is. But so is humble confession when we fail. Our goal must be to balance the aim for resolute obedience with the need to also be vulnerable.

Called to Be Human

I had to learn from experience what Scripture teaches in 1 Thessalonians 2:8: to share the gospel, we must share our life, our real person. If we do not grasp that Christ has freed us to be authentic, we will see evangelism as a project instead of a lifestyle and non-Christians more as objects of our evangelism than as authentic persons.

I remember asking a girl once if she felt comfortable in the area of evangelism. "Oh, yes!" she responded, "I do it twice a week." Somehow it sounded more like taking her multiple vitamins. Evangelism is not just something you "do"—out there—and then get back to "normal" living. Evangelism involves taking people seriously, building a bridge to their island of concerns and needs and then sharing that Christ is Lord in our natural context.

The problem resides, as I have said, in our great difficulty in believing that God is glorified in our utter humanity rather than in our spiritually programmed responses. Most of us fear that who we are inside is just not enough. So we cover up our honest questions and doubts, thinking they would not sound spiritual. Yet this means rejecting our humanness and thus losing our point of authentic contact with the world. We, of all people, should be offering the world a picture of what it means to be truly human. Yet it is often Christians who fear their humanity more than anyone else.

Just as there is confusion concerning what it means to be human, so is there confusion about what it means to be spiritual. We feel it is more spiritual to take our non-Christian friend to a Bible study or to church than to a play or to a film.

Not only do we not understand our natural points of contact with the world, we do not understand our natural points of contact with God himself. He's the one who made us human beings in the first place. He is therefore interested in every aspect of our humanness. We dare not limit him to Bible studies and discussions with Christians. He created life, and he desires to be glorified in the totality of all that adds up to life. And his power and presence will come crashing through to the world as we let him live fully in every aspect of our lives.

Our Model: The Incarnation

Do we have any models for the kind of humanity God intended? Let's turn to the first complete and whole human being who ever lived—Jesus Christ. The word theologians use to describe the event of God coming to us through Christ is the *incarnation*. What is the incarnation? It is the magnificent truth that God came to us through Christ, the Eternal Son of God, and became one of us by assuming human nature while keeping his divine nature. He assumed human form while still remaining himself. Think of it! In his extravagant love, God decided to unite himself to his creation in the closest of all possible unions—*by becoming that which he had created!* Hebrews 1:3 says, "The Son is the radiance of God's glory and the exact representation of his being." In John's Gospel we read, "No one has ever seen God, but God the One and Only, who is at the Father's side, has made him known" (John 1:18).

The reason Christ came to our planet was because sin had separated us from God. Ever since the fall of Adam and Eve, humans have chosen to be centered in themselves instead of centered in God. Sin has separated us from God; sin has separated us from each other; and sin has even separated us from ourselves. Furthermore, sin makes it impossible for us to perceive God accurately. If we are to be reconnected to God, then God must build the bridge back to us. The good news of the gospel is that that is exactly what God did—Christ is our bridge back to God!

But Christ came not only *because* of the sin crisis but also to *resolve* the sin crisis. He took our very sin nature in his body and, through his death, solved the human crisis of sin. The solution had to be from God's side because we lack the power to heal our sin. Only God could and God did!

Have you ever heard a skeptic say, "Isn't it arrogant to claim you know who God is? How could a finite, limited human being ever be confident that he or she has discovered the true God?" I know that was my perspective when I was a young agnostic.

Surprising as it may seem, the doctrine of the incarnation couldn't agree more. The truth is that sin *has* made it impossible for us to know God apart from divine revelation. Without God revealing who he is through Christ, we'd always be wondering if our experience of God was truly an accurate assessment of reality or if our warm, positive feelings toward God might merely be the result of a good digestive track.

Thankfully, God *did* reveal himself through Jesus Christ, and his revelation serves as a model for our evangelism. Jesus told his disciples that "As the Father sent me, so I send you." The key word in that phrase is the *as*. In other words, how did the Father send the Son? We must pay careful attention to how Jesus related to the world because Jesus is our model for how to relate to the world as well. Jesus came to us primarily in five ways: through his birth, life, death, resurrection and ascension. Each aspect of Jesus' life sheds light on evangelism as we shall see.

Jesus' Birth

The birth of Jesus is not simply the emergence of a great man or a religious genius. It marks the moment when eternity crossed into time; when divinity intersected humanity; when Christ, without ceasing to be God, was made man.

Christ's birth offers us a window into understanding God's nature. We see that when Christ came from heaven to earth, the true God did not cling to himself but gave himself away in love, rejoicing to share completely the lives of his creatures. He wasn't stingy like many of the ancient pagan deities. God invested absolutely everything. Christ disclosed the Father's mind and heart because he perfectly embodied all that is in the Father.

Christ's birth also offers us a window into understanding *human* nature. Because the eternal son of God lived a fully human life, he reveals what it means to be human. Since the Enlightenment, we have taken it for granted that human well-being is tied to independence and self-realization. We have thought that happiness comes through throwing off religious shackles and insisting on shaping our own destinies. But Christ shows us that true wholeness and authentic humanity is based not on radical autonomy but on surrender to God's gracious will in our lives. What *dehumanizes* us is to insist on going our own way. Christ lived for his Father's glory by doing his Father's will. Through Christ's actions we observe that it is not our life that matters but our life lost and then rediscovered as God's gift. It is not our freedom that gives us joy but our freedom transformed through our surrender to God. Christ demonstrated that our true freedom and joy come in unity and submission to his Father's will.

But living to please and obey God is not the only thing that makes us authentically human. When God graciously became one of us, he revealed that we are by design, not default, created to depend upon God. Since the beginning of creation, before sin ever entered the picture, Adam and Eve were created to be *God-dependent* creatures, not *self-sufficient* ones. The simple truth is that we are weak and God is strong. But what makes this lesson so painfully difficult for the modern person to accept is that self-sufficiency is considered not a vice but the supreme virtue! Thus we tend to despise our weakness and dependence, while Jesus joyfully accepted his!

Imagine the humility Christ accepted in assuming human nature. What he gave up was immense. He was accustomed to the company of God the Father and holy angels. He enjoyed intimate fellowship within the triune Godhead. In his preincarnate state he participated in creating the world. But once he assumed human nature, he set aside his divine prerogatives. He surrendered his ability to exercise divine power independently. Even if we could offer him the highest splendor the earth affords, his descent would be immense.

Yet he did not enter the human scene born in a palace, nor did he come in the form of a privileged king. The Son of God came to us as a *baby*. His entry could not possibly have been from a greater stance of weakness. For what is weaker or more helpless than a baby?

Not only that, but at Christ's birth the heavens parted and angelic choirs burst into song. Why? Because God, the Creator of all of heaven and earth, was pleased to dwell and be glorified in the Christ child. From the moment of Christ's birth we learn something terribly important: *God is pleased to reveal his glory in the weakness of human form.* Throughout Scripture there is a profound relationship between human weakness and God's power. The apostle Paul said he gloried in his weakness because through its very existence Christ was able to reveal his presence within him (2 Corinthians 11:30; 12:9-10).

When Jesus assumed our human nature, he also assumed human weaknesses. Although he participated in creating the universe, he now needed time alone to pray in order to know his Father's will (Luke 4:42-44). Instead of being self-sufficient, he needed emotional support (Matthew 26:37-38). He also experienced tiredness, thirst and hunger (John 4:6-7).

What does Jesus reveal about what it means to be

human? He shows us that we are created to depend on God's grace and power; our dependence on him is not a result of the Fall. We are God-dependent by nature, and God declares this *good!* Therefore, we must celebrate our smallness, because our human weakness is no hindrance to God.

Too often, though, we don't accept our human form. In all of God's creation we are the only ones who resist our form. Squirrels are not miffed because they are not cats; dogs aren't jealous that they weren't created to be birds; the moon is content not to be the sun. But we are not content with how God made us. Instead, we want to be God. We may not admit it so plainly, but that is truly what lies at the crux of the problem of sin.

Our discontent with ourselves is one of the greatest hindrances to evangelism. I have spent most of my adult life trying to help Christians in the area of evangelism. I have taught and trained Protestant, Orthodox and Catholic Christians on nearly every continent, and over and over again I hear the same comments: "I would witness, but what if I offend? Or what if I'm rejected? What if they ask me a question I can't answer or I blow it when I try to explain what I believe? No, I just can't do it because I'm too unskilled. I need to be better or smarter or more outgoing before God could use me. I just feel so inadequate."

These people are right—we are inadequate! That is precisely the message of the incarnation. But it's a joyous discovery to know that God can use us just as we are. Jesus said, "Blessed are the poor in spirit" (Matthew 5:3). What he means is, "Happy are those who have seen they are not enough." Knowledge of our inadequacy is good news, because only in facing our inadequacy can we see that help is on the way. Only in recognizing that we are *not* enough can we finally turn to the One who *is* enough. Such knowledge should be a source of celebration, not an occasion for angst or shame. God can't help us when we are trying to be more than we really are. But when we face our inadequacy, we open ourselves up to experience God's power, which is magnified in our weakness. In his book *Seeking Peace: Notes and Conversations Along the Way,* author Johann Arnold says:

> The more confidence we have in our own strength and abilities, the less we are likely to have in Christ. Our human weakness is no hindrance to God. In fact, as long as we do not use it as an excuse for sin, it is good to be weak. But this acceptance of weakness is more than acknowledging our limitations. It is experiencing a power much greater than our own and surrendering to it. . . . This is the root of grace—the dismantling of our

power. Whenever even a little power rises up in us, the Spirit and the authority of God will retreat to a corresponding degree. In my estimation this is the single most important insight with regard to the Kingdom of God.

When we say that we won't witness unless we know all the answers to a seeker's questions, or until we have a more well-developed theology, or until we become such skilled communicators that we couldn't possibly offend or be rejected, what is it that we are really saying? Isn't our desire for no-risk, no-error evangelism really a desire for evangelism that doesn't have to depend on God? Our desire to go into evangelistic opportunities armed to the teeth partly stems from the fact that we secretly resent our form. We don't like the fact that we are weak and need to depend on God. Our trouble is that we want to enter situations *as* God—not as human beings who must depend upon God. In doing so we deny the truth of the incarnation. If the Eternal Son of God was willing to come to us as a dependent baby, shouldn't we be willing to let God use us in our weakness as well?

The apostle Paul said, "I came to you in weakness and fear, and with much trembling. My message and my preaching were not with wise and persuasive words, but with a demonstration of the Spirit's power, so that your faith might not rest on men's wisdom but on God's power" (1 Corinthians 2:3-5).

In light of the incarnation, then, if someone asks us a question we can't answer, we are free to say, "That's a great question! I haven't a clue what the answer is, but I can't wait to find out. I'm so glad God brought you into my life to sharpen me intellectually." The incarnation frees us to be ourselves, which in this case means all we have to say is "I don't know!" More important, the incarnation reveals that effective evangelism has little to do with our ability to answer every question. It is *God's* power, *God's* Spirit, *God's* gospel that saves—not our brilliance, knowledge or communication skills. Yes, God has graciously chosen to use us as his vessels. This it why it is vitally important that we share with seekers "not only the gospel but our very lives." But what ultimately matters, the one thing that changes everything, is when God's power works through our weakness.

Billy Graham once described a particular crusade in which he was terribly exhausted:

> I had nothing to give. I had exhausted my material. I had exhausted my body. I had exhausted my mind. Yet the preaching had far more power. It was God taking sheer weakness—it is when I got out of the way and said, "God, You have to do it." I sat on the

platform many nights with nothing to say, nothing. Just sat there. And I knew that in a few minutes I'd have to get up and preach, and I'd just say, "Oh, God, I can't do it!" And yet, I would stand up and all of a sudden it would begin to come . . . just God giving it, that's all. (Quoted in Russ Busby, *Billy Graham: God's Ambassador*)

Likewise we must follow the apostle Paul's example who learned that it was only in coming to the end of *his* own power that Christ was able to reveal his power. Our Lord's words to Paul are also his words to us: "My grace is sufficient for you, for my power is made perfect in weakness" (2 Corinthians 12:9).

Finally, Jesus' birth teaches us that we must be willing to step outside our comfort zone. As we already noted, Jesus came from heaven, so anything earth could offer would be laughable by heaven's standards. Yet Jesus' birth was not in a palace but a manger! He identified not with kings but with the poor. He who was accustomed to the company of his Father and angels was willing to associate with prostitutes and lepers. Talk about getting outside of one's comfort zone! If Jesus left all of heaven to become one of us, shouldn't we at least be willing to get out of our comfort zone as well?

Jesus' Life and Ministry

Jesus' adult life and ministry also reveal crucial principles of evangelism. There was a widely accepted notion among the religious people of Jesus' day that religious activity was what was truly pleasing to God. Jesus smashed that notion. Through both his lifestyle and his teaching, Jesus proclaimed that the primary way to please God was through proper relationships.

Relationships rather than religious activity. Jesus was wholly concerned with God and wholly concerned with people. According to Jesus, the human cause was God's cause. Jesus' lifestyle arose out of the simple truth of loving God, our neighbors and ourselves. His life was a constant celebration of the supreme value, dignity and preciousness of human life.

Establishing relationships then was God's basic strategy for reaching people. When the Word became flesh, God did not send a telegram or shower evangelistic Bible study books from heaven or drop a million bumper stickers from the sky saying, "Smile, Jesus loves you." He sent a man, his Son, to communicate the message. His strategy has not changed. He still sends men and women—before he sends tracts and techniques—to change the world. You may think his strategy is risky, but that is God's problem, not yours.

Jesus had a theology of relationships. Everyone was someone to him. In speaking to the pharisaic lawyer in Luke 10, Jesus sums up all of life in terms of loving relationships—relationships to God, to others and to ourselves. It is far more important that our lives bear the stamp of profound love than religious activity. Jesus implies that people will understand as much of the love of God as they see in our own lives.

We are called to mirror the love of God—a love so extravagant that we must never keep it to ourselves. Why did Jesus so stress and demonstrate the necessity of a life reflecting the stamp of profound love? Jesus said such a life reveals his Father's essence. When we love God with all of our heart, soul and mind and we love our neighbor as ourselves, we are actually reflecting the deepest reality of all—the reality of the Trinity. God is a relational being. His very essence is of three persons in union. We have been created as relational beings, because we are made in his image. God's outgoing love is part of his essence that we are to reflect. Therefore we must never treat people as evangelistic projects. The question we must ask ourselves in light of Jesus' ministry is this: Do we have a real, authentic friendship with at least one unbeliever? Or are our lives more accurately described as being members of the Holy Huddle?

Radical identification, radical difference. But if the kingdom of God is about establishing relationships of love, then how are we to relate to others without compromising our own witness? Yes, we know that Jesus entered the muddy waters of the Jordan to be identified in baptism with the poor, the sinful and the needy. We know that Jesus entered into the human trenches of human experience. But he was also God! How do *we* enter the messy lives of others without moral compromise?

This is a crucial question if we are to be an effective witness. I think Jesus loved and changed the world in two ways: by his *radical identification* with men and women and by his *radical difference*. Jesus responded to people first by noticing what they had in common (John 4:7). But it was often in the context of their similarities that Jesus' difference came crashing through (John 4:10).

Jesus was sleeping in a boat when a furious storm came up. What could be more human than the act of sleeping to restore one's body? Yet when the disciples became terrified that they would drown, they woke him. Jesus rebuked the storm: "Quiet! Be still!" But the disciples were still terrified: "Who is this? Even the wind and the waves obey him!" (Mark 4:39, 41).

It was as people discovered Jesus' profound humanness that they began to recognize his deity.

God's holiness became shattering and penetrating as Jesus confronted people on his very own level of humanity. But the point is that it took both his radical identification and his radical difference to change the world. So it will be for us.

How did Christ radically identify with others? Jesus was a remarkably open man. He did not think it was unspiritual for him to share his physical needs (John 4:7). He did not fear weakening his testimony by asking for the emotional and prayerful support of his friends in the Garden of Gethsemane. Here is our model for genuine godliness—and we see him asking for support and desiring others to minister to him.

People in Jesus' day thought holy men could only be found in synagogues, but Jesus' work was in the marketplace. He went to weddings, to parties, and dined with quite unsavory characters. He enjoyed people. He made people feel welcome. He cared deeply about people and wasn't afraid to show it. The Stoics (a Greek school of philosophy that emphasized self-control and maintaining dominance over the emotions) were proud of concealing their tears, but Jesus didn't conceal his. He wept openly whether for a city or for a friend's loss. Children loved him. Adults were affected so much by him that some just wanted to touch his clothes. Why? Because they saw that

Jesus loved them. His love was extravagant, never cautious or timid. And he talked of his Father's *endless* love. Jesus treated others in such a way that said, people may be lost, broken and damaged by sin, but that doesn't mean they have no worth or they aren't loved in God's eyes.

We must learn to relate transparently and lovingly to others because that is God's style of relating to us. Jesus commands us to go and then preach—not to preach and then leave. We are not to shout the gospel from a safe and respectable distance, remaining uninvolved. We must open our lives enough to let people see that we laugh and hurt and cry too. That is where I would fault my "torpedo" evangelist. She violated an incarnation understanding of reality. I was merely an evangelistic project; I was not a person to be related to with dignity and genuine care. Can you imagine Jesus doing such a thing? Can you picture Jesus throwing a gospel spitball to the woman at the well in John 4, saying, "God bless! But don't come near. Your life is just too messy!" If Jesus left all heaven and glory to become one of us, shouldn't we at least be willing to leave our dorm room or church or Bible study circle to reach out to a friend?

Even as we identify with our unbelieving friends, however, we must remember that Jesus called his disciples to be different as well. We must never try to escape from the truth that there is a fundamental difference between Christians and non-Christians. If we ignore or minimize this difference, we will be of little use to God or to the world.

How will our radical difference be expressed? The tension lies between identifying with the world and loving it as deeply as Jesus did (being similar to the world), and yet obeying Jesus' prayer that we would be different from the world (John 17:16). We must remember that identification with the world does not equal being *identical* to the world. If we seek to understand the world but live exactly as non-Christians do, no impact will be made. Only as we identify with the world while living Spirit-filled lives will revolution take place. That means our daily time alone with God will be critical to our evangelism, for it will change us into the likeness of Christ. Persistent prayer is equally vital—we must learn that to truly love our friends with the love of Christ, we must pray for them daily, asking Christ to display his love to us and through us.

Jesus tells us that we are salt and light (Matthew 5:13-16). Our difference will be seen in our Christian character, by the fact that we are being conformed to God's moral teaching, by our devotion and love for God, by the fact that we do not judge others but serve them and by our whole-hearted commitment to obeying Christ as Lord.

The tension of being holy and human as God intended will never be easy. We will have to be guided and empowered by the Holy Spirit and God's Word for our every situation. But our lives must bear the same dual stance to the world: radically identified in love and radically different in holiness.

Jesus' Death

What can we learn from Jesus' death that will help us as we witness? I explore the theme of the cross in greater depth in another book in this series called *The Way of Jesus*. However, one of the questions I am frequently asked when I give evangelism training conferences is "How do you evaluate success in evangelism? Does it mean I have failed when my friend doesn't accept Christ? I feel so discouraged when I don't see positive results."

My answer is twofold. First, our task is to *expose* people to the gospel, not to *impose*. Only the Spirit of God can change a person's heart. We could not convert a person if our life depended on it. It is God's power alone that causes someone who is dead to sin to become alive to God. Therefore we must remind ourselves that we aren't responsible for the results. Rather we are called to be faithful, to share the good news through our words and deeds, and at the appropriate time, under the guidance of the Spirit, we may ask the person if he or she is ready to receive Christ. But the results we leave with God.

Yet how do we cope with our discouragement when we do not see the results we pray and long for? We must reflect on the cross. There will be times in life when evil appears to be winning and we are tempted to think that because we can see everything that evil is accomplishing, God must therefore be doing nothing. It isn't true! The cross reveals that the darkest moment of human history turned out to be the greatest victory. God used the most heinous act ever committed on this planet to accomplish the greatest good. We must not forget when we are discouraged that God always has the last word. His purposes cannot be thwarted. We must not allow Satan to discourage us.

I have seen some people come to Christ in a seemingly short period of time; others, like my own father, took over thirty years; still others I have prayed for have shown no interest. Our job is to keep praying, to not lose heart, to ask for patience and to remember that only God converts the human soul.

When we meditate on the cross, we become

aware that "while we were yet sinners Christ died for us" (Romans 5:8). This means that even the most loathsome or unlikely person is not beyond the reach of the cross. We can never look at anyone and conclude that he or she is a hopeless case. If Christ died for us, it means he loves us. We need to see people through the love of the cross.

I recently spoke in a church in California and a member shared the inspiring story of his conversion with me. I am including it to show just one example of the miraculous way God works to bring people to himself.

A Personal Account:
One Life Transformed

When I was in the Navy I was a member of the "hole gang" (engine room crew). We were probably the most lowly workers on the entire ship, living in the bowels of the ship with high-pressure, superheated steam. We always figured we were pretty much written off if the thing ever went down due to combat damage.

In 1978, while we were overseas on the USS *Dubuque,* an amphibious assault ship with a crew of 425 sailors that hauled around 2,500 marines and all their toys, a new electronics technician named Dutch came. (He was housed in the air-conditioned quiet, up in the radar section.) One of few Christians on that ship, he evidently began praying and looking for a way to reach others. His prayer partner was another one of the electronics technicians. The two of them thought that there had to be a way to take the ship for God. The Lord let them know they had to reach the most un-godly group aboard to really speak to others. To do this they started to pray for the salvation of just one hole-gang sailor.

The Lord provided not only one but three very drug dependent guys. These fellows had habits that needed to be satisfied immediately upon rising, through the day and right before going to sleep. All three not only accepted God's grace through Jesus, but they each experienced total release from their habits and desires for the crazy lifestyles they had been living. They became on-fire Christians not only in word but in deed. These five then sought out and witnessed to everyone they came across about the dramatic change that God had brought to their lives. Through this witness, I would estimate that somewhere between 33 percent and 50 per-cent of the ship's company became Christians.

I had grown up in the church but had rejected its teaching due to personal issues with a pastor in my family's church. I had decided that God was not real and that there was nothing there worth clinging to. However, when I saw the change in these three close friends of mine, I had no choice but to acknowledge that God was not only real but very much involved in our daily affairs, and I too gave my heart to him.

◆　◆　◆

When we are reminded of God's grace to us through the cross, we must ask ourselves, *Who are the "impossible cases" I must begin to pray for?*

Jesus' Resurrection

Not one of the disciples ever imagined that he would see Jesus after death. There could not have been a more depressed group of people after Christ's death than Jesus' followers. They must have asked themselves over and over, *Why did he insist on dying? Why did he choose this senseless strategy? He should have withdrawn for a while and let things cool off. Anyone could have escaped the guards. But Jesus deliberately gave himself over to them. Now he is dead. We saw him perform miracles, set our hearts on fire with truth, give us hope and purpose as we had never known before. And now he lies there, still and cold, unable to help anyone.*

But then the disciples saw Jesus, risen, standing radiant, stretching out his hands to them. What was their response? They were terrified. They thought they were hallucinating! Yet what they saw and came to believe is that it was truly him.

What does the resurrection of Christ teach us about evangelism? First, never underestimate God. We worship the God of the impossible! It was the Spirit of God that raised Jesus from the dead, that made the amino acids rekindle and the corpse sit up, that revitalized brain-dead cells and restored breath to collapsed lungs and made him live. Therefore we must never look at anyone and say, "God could never reach that person." The resurrection proves that what is impossible for humans is possible for God. If the Spirit of God could raise Christ from physical death and give him life, then he can take us who are dead to sin and make us alive to God. Determine to see everyone through the eyes of the resurrection power and potential of God! We must always remember that if God had the power to reach us, then he has the power to reach anyone, for we are all impossible cases.

Second, our evangelism is revitalized when we see that the power that raised Jesus from the dead is the same power that is given to us when we receive Christ. It is the Holy Spirit who works with us and through us as we engage in the task of evangelism. It is the Spirit of God that opens blind eyes, convicts seekers of sin, nudges them to commitment and brings about their transformation when they receive Christ. What enables us to live the Christian life, to witness effectively and to benefit from the means of grace is the power unleashed by Christ's rising from the dead. He did more than die and pay the penalty of sin. He was raised from death itself, and the very power God used to raise him is the power made available to us. Therefore we need to tap into that power as we learn how to walk in the Spirit. We must learn that living in the resurrection is living in the old world by the energy of the new world to come!

How do we tap into the spiritual resources God has given? Prayer is one example of an indispensable spiritual tool that fortifies us to tell others about the good news. We pray for blind eyes to be opened. Many people are blinded to the gospel. We need to pray that the Spirit of God will open the eyes of the blind so they can understand the truth about Jesus.

James Fraser, an English missionary among the Lisu of Southwest China, worked tirelessly for years without seeing any conversions. But then revival came in an extraordinary way. Fraser did not attribute the spectacular success of his mission to his energetic evangelism or his wise counsel. He believed it was his emphasis on prayer in his own life and his gift of fostering prayer groups back in his homeland that made the astonishing difference. He enlisted constant prayer from others, giving these prayer groups back home remarkable details, and asking them to pray for thirty minutes a day if they could. He felt it was this prayer support that protected his work from the satanic stronghold that existed in the remote mountain range where he worked, and it contributed to the thousands who were eventually converted. In the book *Behind the Ranges* Fraser has written in fascinating detail on what it means to pray a prayer of faith, how to take a stand of faith on ground we believe God has given and how to fight and resist Satan in the name of Christ.

How God Helped Me with Bob

I remember bumping into an old friend I hadn't seen since high school. As we sat looking at a dinner menu, this friend, Bob, asked me if there had been any significant changes in my life since high school. I took a deep breath and began to tell him about my faith in Christ. I remembered him as being intelligent and cynical, and it soon became apparent that in those respects he hadn't changed.

I tried every approach I could think of, only to be rebuffed with polite but patronizing remarks. Knowing I was getting nowhere fast, I excused myself to go to the restroom. There I prayed a fervent prayer: "Lord, all Bob is hearing is *blah-blah-blah*. Let my words be spoken in the power of your

Spirit. Transmit through me your meaning and speak to his heart. Open his eyes, Lord."

I returned to the table. A few minutes later, in response to a question he asked me, I began telling Bob my conversion story. Initially he listened with the same skepticism. But suddenly it was as if someone had reached inside his head and turned on a light. Bob's whole countenance changed. In fact, he had a look of astonishment. "Wait a minute, that makes sense," he said. He began peppering me with questions about the Bible, about Jesus, about the meaning of the cross. We left the meal several hours later with my challenging him to start reading the Gospels.

The next morning the phone rang. It was Bob saying he'd been up all night and only had the Gospel of John left to read. Soon I introduced Bob to Christian men who befriended him and invited him to a Bible discussion. Six months later Bob gave his life to Christ.

How did it happen? It became clear to me after getting reacquainted with Bob that God had been pursuing him for a long time. Yet I know of no other explanation for what happened in that restaurant other than that the Spirit of God responded to my prayer. Why Bob responded to prayer so quickly, while others I have prayed for have not, is a mystery. But that experience powerfully reinforced for me how vital prayer is to evangelism. We need God's power to do God's work. We need to ask God to give us wisdom, effectiveness and renewed faith, but above all we need to ask him to open the eyes and soften the hearts of those he is seeking. Eugene Peterson, in his book *A Long Obedience in the Same Direction,* writes, "The Bible is not a script for a funeral service, but it is the record of God always bringing life where we expected to find death. Everywhere it is the story of resurrection."

Jesus' Ascension

What does the ascension of Christ teach us about witnessing? In the book of Acts, Luke describes Jesus' parting words as he gave the disciples their commission: "But you will receive power when the Holy Spirit comes on you; and you will be my witnesses in Jerusalem, and in all Judea and Samaria, and to the ends of the earth" (Acts 1:8). Then Jesus was taken up before their eyes while they stared intently up into the sky. Suddenly two angels appeared and said, "Men of Galilee . . . why do you stand here looking into the sky? This same Jesus, who has been taken from you into heaven, will come back in the same way you have seen him go into heaven" (Acts 1:11).

In other words, the angels were implying that

the disciples could not bring Jesus back by gazing up into the sky. He had gone, and they must let him go; he will return in his own time and in the same way. Therefore, since Jesus' words were to go to the end of the earth as his witnesses, their calling was to be witnesses not stargazers. It was the earth, not the sky, which was to be their preoccupation. The vision they were given from Jesus was not upward in a nostalgic remembrance of the good times past, but outward in compassion to a lost world that needed him. It is the same for us. We have work to do in the power of the Spirit.

Furthermore, Christ's commission was to all his followers. The biblical text does not read, "Go ye therefore all extroverts, all with the gift of evangelism and all Baptists. As for the rest of you, just be sure to go to conferences and worship regularly." No, the call is to all Christ's followers, whether we have the gift of evangelism or not. That is one of the interesting aspects of God's gifting. Not all of us are called to be prophets or teachers or evangelists, but *everyone* is called to be a witness regardless of the nature of our gifts. Christ's call to witness is a command not an option. The question isn't *if* but only *how*.

Furthermore, when the two angels spoke to the disciples and basically told them to quit looking up at heaven and start focusing on the work they were called to do on earth, it was in effect a warning. If they focused only on heaven, they would be guilty of a false pietism. Yet aren't many Christians guilty of this very thing? I often meet believers who live as if the only purpose of life is to enjoy fellowship with Jesus. Yet that violates the commission Jesus gave. We are not to live as if we are already in heaven; we are to live as if we are on earth, which means getting our priorities in alignment with God. One of God's purposes is to seek and save the lost. Jesus makes it clear that there will come a time when it's too late. When he returns, the time for salvation will be past. Therefore, let us be about our Father's business!

Collected Clues

In light of what we have learned from the incarnation, are there any more tips that will help us as we witness? If you are waiting to make contact with people around you, representing Jesus Christ to them, here are some collected clues that may help.

Be yourself—plus. Let God make you fully you. Rejoice in your God-given temperament, and use it for God's purposes. God made some of us shy, others outgoing. We should praise him for that. If you are shy, remember that your shyness is not an excuse to avoid relationships—rather it is a means to love the world in a different way than an extrovert.

I get discouraged when I hear people say that it is easy for me to evangelize because I am outgoing. Being an extrovert *is not* the essential tool in evangelism—obedience and love and the empowerment of God's Spirit are. There are many people I could never reach, and would probably only intimidate, because I am outgoing. God will have to use other Christians to reach them. But I do not feel guilty about it, because I have learned that God is not glorified by my living life with someone else's personality. I must be who I am created to be. And I must reach out to others in a way that is both sensitive to the person with whom I am talking and consistent with my own personality.

But regardless of our temperaments, we all must become initiators. More and more I see that the mark of mature Christians is whether they choose to be the "hosts" or the "guests" in relationships. Christians must be the ones who love, care and listen first. We can all take initiative, whether in a quiet or more conspicuous way.

Be a risk-taker. Taking initiative opens us up to the risk of rejection. Letting people inside our lives is a frightening but essential ingredient in evangelism. We also take a risk when we leave our security blankets in order to penetrate *their* lives.

Once I was walking through O'Hare Airport in Chicago when my purse slipped and everything tumbled out. As I was stuffing things back inside, a young woman stopped to ask the time. Then she nervously bit her lip and asked, "You don't know where I could get a drink, do you?" I didn't. But as I searched her face, I saw that she was distraught. So I stood up and started a conversation. She quickly interrupted with, "Do you know how much a drink would cost here?"

I could see we were getting nowhere, and suddenly I heard myself saying, "Gee, I don't know, but would you like me to go with you to find out?"

"Oh, would you? I would really love the company," she responded.

Off we went, and all the way I was kicking myself for it—here I was wandering around an airport with a perfect stranger. How unorthodox! Then I thought, *I wonder what Jesus would do in a situation like this?* I realized that he would probably be more concerned about *why* she needed the drink than about going into a bar. I knew that if I could not be at ease around her when she had a drink in her hand, and allow God to lead me into what *he* perceived as a mission field, then I would not be very effective in communicating God's unconditional love.

After we found a restaurant, it took only minutes before she began sharing that she had decided to leave her husband. Her husband, unaware of her decision, would be meeting her at the airport in Michigan. She was petrified at facing his response and felt totally alone. "Oh, but it's ridiculous telling this to a complete stranger— how boring this must be for you," she would comment and then talked on.

The saddest part was her inability to believe anyone could care for her. She trusted no one. When at one point she mentioned a problem I told her I could identify with, she said, "Oh, so that's why you act as if you care. Listen, aren't you afraid of picking up strangers like me? You really should be more careful." As I began to tell her who God was and that he was the one who brought me into situations like this, she seemed mesmerized.

Soon we were walking to her plane, but I felt torn inside. I wanted to reach out to her and tell her how moved I was by her problems, and that there was a God who cared deeply for her. But she was so cold and defensive that I feared her rejection. Finally at the gate I took her hand and said, "Listen, I want you to know that I really care about you, and I'll be praying for you the minute you get off the plane." She just stared blankly at me. Then, turning away, she said, "Um . . . I'm sorry—I just don't know how to handle love," and walked away.

The encounter was not a smashing success, but I felt I was obedient. Being a Christian means taking risks: risking that our love will be rejected, misunderstood or even ignored. Now I am not suggesting that you race to your local bar for Jesus. But if you find yourself in a situation in which you believe God has put you, then so long as it does not tempt you to sin, nor has it been a problem area for you in the past, then accept the risk for his love's sake.

See beneath the crust. Once we have taken the risk to make contact with a person, we must never assume that he or she won't be open to Christianity. Once we get beneath the surface of a person, we will usually discover a sea of needs. We must learn how to interpret those needs correctly, as Jesus did. Jesus was not turned off by needs— even needs wrongly met—because they told him something about the individual.

The Samaritan woman had had five husbands and was currently living with a sixth man. The disciples took one look at her and felt, *That woman? Become a Christian? No way. Why, just look at her lifestyle!* But Jesus looked at the very same lifestyle and came to the opposite conclusion. What Jesus saw in her frantic male-hopping was not just a loose woman. It was not her human need for tenderness that alarmed Jesus, but rather the way she sought to meet that need. Even more, Jesus saw that her need indicated a real hunger for God. He seemed to be saying to the disciples, "Look at what potential she has for God. See how hard she is trying to find the right thing in all the wrong places."

That blows the lid right off evangelism for me. How many Samaritan men and women do you know? Everywhere I am I see people frantically looking for the right things in all the wrong places. The tragedy is that so often my initial response is to withdraw and assume they will never become Christians. Yet God has shown me that they are usually the ones who are most open. We must ask ourselves, *How do I interpret the needs and lifestyles of my friends? Do I look at their drinking or drug habits or their sleeping around or their obsession with false values and say, 'That's wrong' and walk away? Or do I penetrate their mask and discover why they do this in the first place? And then do I try to love them where they are?*

We can show people that they are right to want to fill the void, and then they may be joyfully surprised to discover that the emptiness inside is, as Pascal describes it in his *Pensées,* a "God-shaped vacuum."

Breaking Through the Stereotypes

We must not become, as John Stott puts it, "rabbit-hole Christians." For example, we can sometimes see this at work in the college context. Collegiate rabbit-hole Christians are the kind who pop their heads out of the hole, leave their Christian roommates in the morning and scurry to class, only to frantically search for a Christian to sit next to (an odd way to approach a mission field!). Thus they proceed from class to class. When dinner time comes, they sit with all the Christians in their dorm at one huge table and think, *What a witness!* From there they go to their all-Christian Bible study, and they might even catch a prayer meeting where the Christians pray for the nonbelievers on their floor. (But what luck that they were able to live on the only floor with seventeen Christians!) Then at night they scurry back to their Christian roommates. Safe! They made it through the day, and their only contacts with the world were those mad, brave dashes to and from Christian activities.

What a complete reversal of the biblical command to be salt and light to the world! Rabbit-hole Christians remain insulated and isolated from the world when they are commanded to penetrate it. How can we be the salt of the earth if we never get out of the saltshaker?

Christians, however, are not the only ones to blame for this phenomenon. The tragedy is that even the world encourages our isolationism. Have you ever wondered why everyone always "behaves" when the minister joins a television talk show? Suddenly their language changes and their behavior improves. Why? They want to do their part to keep the Reverend feeling holy. They will play the religious game while he is around because he needs to be protected from that cold, real world out there.

Sometimes non-Christians will act oddly around us because they are genuinely convicted by the Holy Spirit in us—and that is good. But all too often they are behaving differently because they feel that is the way they are supposed to act around religious types.

I am often put in a religious box when people discover what my profession is. During my single days when I ministered to collegiates, I had a "clergy card" that sometimes enabled me to travel at reduced rates. The only problem was that occasionally ticket agents did not believe I was authorized to use it! A young female just wasn't what they had in mind when they saw a clergy card. More than once I have been asked, "Okay, honey, now where did you rip this off?"

The funniest case occurred when I was flying

from San Francisco to Portland. I arrived at the counter and was greeted by an exceedingly friendly male ticket agent.

"Well, hello-o-o there!" he said.

"Uh . . . I'd like to pick up my ticket to Portland, please."

"Gee, I'm sorry—you won't be able to fly there tonight."

"Why—is the flight canceled?"

"No, it's because you're going out with me tonight."

"What?"

"Listen, I know this great restaurant with a hot band. You'll never regret it."

"Oh, I'm sorry; I really must get to Portland. Do you have my ticket?"

"Aw, what's the rush? I'll pick you up at 8:00 . . ."

"Look, I really must go to Portland," I said.

"Well, okay. Too bad though. Hey, I can't find your ticket. Looks like it's a date then!"

"Oh, I forgot to tell you, it's a . . . special ticket," I said.

"Oh, is it youth fare?"

"No, um, well, it's . . . ah, *clergy,*" I whispered as I leaned over the counter.

He froze. "What did you say?"

"It's clergy."

"CLERGY!" he yelled, as the entire airport looked our way. His face went absolutely pale, and you could tell he was horrified by only one thought, *Oh no, I flirted with that nun!*

When he disappeared behind the counter, I could hear him whisper in horror to the other ticket agent a few feet away, "Hey, George, get a load of that woman up there, she's *clergy.*" Suddenly another man rose from behind the counter, smiled and nodded and disappeared again. I never have felt so religious in my entire life. As I stood there trying to look as secular as possible, my ticket agent reappeared and stood back several feet behind the desk. Looking a bit shaken and sounding like a tape recording he said, "Good afternoon. We certainly hope there have been no inconveniences. And on behalf of our airline, we'd like to wish you a very safe and pleasant flight . . . Sister Manley."

As humorous as this incident was, I think it shows how difficult it is to maintain our authenticity before the world. The challenge is to not allow ourselves to become more or less than human.

Christians should be positive! We cannot overestimate the importance of our attitude. Our attitude and style communicate content just as our words. If we notice that non-Christians seem embarrassed, apologetic and defensive, it is probably because they are picking up *our* attitude. If we assume they will be intrigued to discover the true nature of Christianity, they probably will! If we communicate enthusiasm, not defensiveness, and carefully listen instead of sounding like a recording of "Answers to Questions You Didn't Happen to Ask," non-Christians will become intrigued.

Learn also to identify with their defenses against Christianity. When talking with an intellectual professor, for example, we have every right to say, "I think one of the hardest issues a Christian must face is how in the world we know that it is true. Are we deluding ourselves and worshiping on the basis of need rather than truth?" In that way we can free seekers to feel at home with us. Walls are torn down and bridges built when we suggest the objections they may have.

Finally, as you approach relationships with non-Christians, look for ways in which God made you alike. The apostle Paul looked for points he had in common with others and began building from there (see Acts 17:22).

I once lived in an apartment above a woman who could only be described as a real swinger. She had just moved in, and every time I saw her she would be on her way to another party. We always exchanged friendly words and one day she said, "Becky, I like you. You're all right. Let's get together next week and smoke a joint, okay?" I replied, "Gee, thanks! I really like you too, and I'd love to spend time with you. Actually I can't stand the stuff, but I'd sure love to do something else. See you later!"

Of course she looked a bit surprised, not so much because I did not do drugs but because I had expressed real appreciation at the thought of spending time with her. I could have told her, "Excuse me! I am a Christian and I never touch the stuff," but I wanted to affirm whatever I possibly could first, without selling short the standards of a Christian. Too often we broadcast what we "don't do" when we should be trying to discover genuine points of contact.

Explaining the Gospel

First, *investigate*. We need to learn how to be listeners before we begin to proclaim the gospel. Listening is like rowing around an island, carefully studying the shoreline for an appropriate landing place. We explore our non-Christian friends' religious and family backgrounds, cultural interests, needs, dreams and fears. It is amazing to me that we spend fortunes so that missionaries can learn foreign languages, while it never occurs to us that we must "learn the language" of our friends at home. We must get inside their thought processes

and understand their questions. Don't leap to resolve every question; raise some! (God does that
all the time in Scripture.)

Next, *stimulate*. Once we have some idea of
who we are talking to, we must learn to arouse
their curiosity about the gospel. I think this is one
of the most neglected aspects of evangelism. We
try to saturate people with the light before we
have caught their attention. In Acts 26:18 Christ
calls Paul *first* to open the eyes of the unbelieving
Gentiles, *before* he helped them turn from dark-
ness to light. He was called to arouse their interest
so they would want to hear his message. We must
learn to be "fishers of men" and not "hunters of
men." We need to look at Paul and Jesus to study
their fishing techniques.

Jesus was often deliberately vague with people
at first, not giving the whole answer until he had
their complete interest. He knew that the Samaritan woman (John 4:7) would not have a clue
about what "living water" meant, any more than
Nicodemus (John 3:1) would comprehend the
term "born again." Jesus was deliberately obscure
to see if they had any spiritual interest and, if so,
to enhance it. Paul aroused the curiosity of the
Thessalonian Jews in the synagogue with his
fierce logic and rational arguments (Acts 17:3-4).
At Areopagus he captured the interest of the

Greeks with his ability to use their secular poets to affirm his point (Acts 17:28). We too must develop a style of intriguing evangelism—not only through our conversation, but also in our love for each other, our personal godliness and our genuine concern for non-Christians.

Finally, *relate*. Once we have discovered where people are and have aroused their interest in what we have to say, we are ready to relate the gospel message. Steps one and two are the necessary pre-evangelistic steps that will enable us to communicate Christ more effectively. But it is not enough to take the first two steps without the third. Paul, for example, knew his audience, found where they needed to grapple with commitment, and then proclaimed the gospel (Acts 17:16-34).

Notice that Paul's message contained content and not just experience. Somehow it is difficult to imagine Paul on top of Areopagus defending his faith before secular philosophers by saying, "Gee, I dunno fellas, it's just this feeling in my heart." Along with our experience, we need a clear explanation of the gospel. If you want to see different ways to clearly communicate the gospel, check in the back of my book *Out of the Saltshaker*. And you'll find the gospel presented through story and Scripture in my booklet *The Way of Jesus,* which is appropriate to give to a seeker. We must resist the trend to make Jesus sound more like a happy pill to be popped than a Lord to be obeyed at any cost.

Fully Human

We have said that Jesus modeled a way of relating to the world that both radically identified with it and radically differed from it. I think our most radical difference will be felt when we live as we were created to be—fully human. Jesus has shown us that the most essential ingredient of true humanity is the freedom to respond totally, completely and passionately to God. If we let God make us authentic humans—not subcultural Christians, but affirming, vulnerable, open people who penetrate the world and love it as deeply as Jesus did—then the presence of God will be overwhelmingly felt by the world.

It cost God everything to identify with the nature of humanity. So will it cost us a great deal to identify and walk alongside our seeker friends. To give the message is easy. To give our lives is costly. But it is the giving of our lives for Christ's sake that changes the world, for it authenticates the message that we preach. God asks for nothing less.

Other books by Rebecca Manley Pippert

Out of the Saltshaker

"Christians and non-Christians have something in common. We're all uptight about evangelism." So begins the bestselling book now considered a modern classic on evangelism. Through biblical insight, wit and wisdom, stories and plain common sense, The author helps us feel relaxed and enthusiastic about sharing our faith. This thoroughly revised and expanded edition is now more valuable than ever with added material on meeting the complex challenges of witnessing to Christ in our postmodern age. *288 pp., 2220-8*

Hope Has Its Reasons

This is a book geared for people who want honest answers to honest questions. The author examines the persistently human longings that all of us share about significance, meaning, life and truth, and the search for security. Only after she unravels the core of the real problem that plagues us does she explore how Christ can meet our longings and solve our human crisis. There are no canned formulas or saccharine clichés. Realism rings in the stories she tells and the ideas she pursues. In doing so she leads us beyond the search for our own significance to the reasons for our hope in discovering God. *197 pp., 2278-X*

A Heart for God

How can God use the difficulties and sufferings in our lives to build character and deepen our faith? The biblical David faced some desperate circumstances and some tough choices. So do we, day by day. The author shows us how God is able to use the everyday grit and glory of our lives to shape a holy life within us. Using David as her guide she helps us understand the way Christian virtue is developed in our souls and vices are rooted out. We learn how we, like David, can choose the good, overcome temptation and grow to be one who has a heart for God. *236 pp., 2341-7*

Transformation

Would you like to move from despair to hope? Would you like to transform your feelings of fear to faith? Would you like to turn envy into compassion? The Bible shows how David turned these negative emotions in his life into godly character qualities. In this Christian Basics Bible Study, based on the Bible's account of David and the book *A Heart for God,* you'll investigate David's life, choices, mistakes and triumphs. Then you'll discover how you can make the same transformation in your own life. *6 studies, 2019-1*

Evangelism

"I don't want to offend people." "I don't know what to say." Most of us can think of at least one hundred reasons not to share the gospel. Evangelism can be intimidating. But it can also be a natural and exciting way of life. These Bible studies, written for Christians, will help you discover creative ways to share the gospel in your everyday situations and surroundings. *12 studies, 3050-2*

An Evangelism Tool Kit
by Rebecca Manley Pippert

What Is It?	What Do I Do with It?	Why?
Talking About Jesus Without Sounding Religious	Read it.	Learn to overcome your fears and effectively share your faith.
How to Lead a Seeker Bible Discussion	Use it.	Learn to lead an effective seeker Bible study.
Looking at the Life of Jesus	Study it.	Here's the material for everyone to use in your seeker Bible discussion!
The Way of Jesus	Give it away.	A perfect gift for seekers who want to go deeper.

For more information on Rebecca Pippert's training
conferences through Saltshaker Ministries, or for helpful
hints on leading seeker studies, visit her website at
<www.saltshaker.org>.